BANDIT/QUEEN

THE RUNAWAY STORY OF
BELLE STARR

BANDIT/QUEEN

THE RUNAWAY STORY OF BELLE STARR

POEMS BY MARGOT DOUAIHY

ILLUSTRATIONS BY BRI HERMANSON

CLEMSON
UNIVERSITY
PRESS

Published by Clemson University Press in Clemson, South Carolina.

This book is set in Adobe Minion Pro.

For information about Clemson University Press,
please visit our website at www.clemson.edu/press.

Library of Congress Control Number: 2022937117

TABLE OF CONTENTS

❊

❊

Poems

Plates

✦

As the only woman among the outlaws,
she was not chained as the others were.
This would prove to be a mistake.

—JONITA MULLINS

I regard myself as a woman who has seen much of life.

—BELLE STARR

ARCHIVE

Life of Famed Belle Starr, a Carthage Native,
Was Colorful & Full of Trouble

||

Consider the slight hunch in the back. The crop in her hand.

||

Famous Woman Outlaw & Desperado

||

The Dashing & Daring Belle

||

Handy gal with a six-shooter, a sure shot
who never forgot an injury or forgave a foe,
a terror to those she hated & false friends.

||

Consider the tilt of the head. The countenance,
the ghost blur, the haunted look of a hunter.

||

The weathered face belied by the voice,
raised ever so slightly, like a scar.

||

The silent scrape of the star as it falls to earth.

[FIG. 1] WOMAN OF MYSTERY, BELLE STARR, ARMED & ELEGANT.

WILD

riding toward it
or   away   Look!
       does it matter?
would it be better
if I were sadder?
less joyous? less   in lust
with the vicious lift
wild   unsewn   unknown
a hunger that cannot
be owned   or named
        staring down
the barrel   quick kiss
before dying   Look!

      dots stop

Pounding Pounding Pounding Pounding
the way
a hammer
inside
the piano
hits
the
string

O how she plays

tried   even the most feral
even if you   animal knows how
                              to pretend
      you couldn't stop it   it's dead
                              to live again

Don't look!   now now now now now now now no no no no no no no no now   She's ~~behind~~ you

ALIAS

Belle Starr, Starr Belle, Myra Belle Shirley, Myra Maybelle
Shirley Starr, Queen of the Bandits, Bandit Queen, Female
Desperado, Female Jesse James, Female Robin Hood,
Fugitive, Ruthless Huntress, Bloodthirsty Madwoman
Supreme, Mistress of the Outlaws, Desperate Woman,
Dangerous Woman, Daring Woman, Dashing Female
Highwayman, Criminal, Moll, Bellissima Starr, Cleopatra
of West Country, Petticoat Terror of the Plains, Vile Reptile,
Villain, Vixen, Valorous Female Gentry, Mother, Mother
Who Brushed Her Children's Hair Too Harshly, Unholy
Bitch With One Purple Eye & One Coal-Black Eye She Will
Hypnotize You So Look Away Look AWAY!!!!!!!!!!!!!!!!!!,
Kinder Than My Own Kin, Never Did I Meet a More
Generous Soul

HEIST

Almost too easy in a world of too hard—

horse theft!—a crime as sweet—to me at least—

as plucking a plump tomato from a twitching vine—

the taking, not as much fun as the stakeout—

stalking the field, stealthy choreography—

why act surprised? I've earned my place in the lineage—

bastards just fine with a bat or bullet to the head—

thieves, conmen, confederates—torn maps—

uncivil war. Father's Southern "sympathy." I'll free myself—
         (~~thank you very much~~)

I'll steal horses for dresses, & you'll call me a whore—

but you do the same, Sir, for smokes, women, & drink—

Some jacked up thinkin' if you ask me. Nobody dare ask.

&&&

The farm hands talk back
as they walk with dented buckets.

Bats like bags of acid, sprites
of dynamite, dive sideways.

Watch me disappear reappear smear
the air like a seizure of tornado shadows.

Dang! You missed it! The dance, the game,
woodsmoke in my hair. Flash of tremors.

Rippling flesh after the rapture,

                coming

                        or leaving.   Your stallion's gone.

I steal horses because they're there. Because I can.

&&&

So, there was one time I took ownership of a mare
to save her from a wayward dæmon

who was starving her slowly, her ribs
severe as prison bars before a hanging.

Should have shot the creep in the eye
when I could. Hesitation is weak.

Reliable? Sure, I am that. But an obedient woman?
No. That path was never for me.

No regrets, save for not rustling more ponies,
hustling more feckless men.

The cuckold cannot stand Venus's prints
in the dirt, only sign I was there.

I'm taking your horse & giving you the gift
of the ghost. You'll never be alone.

In & gone before you realize you've been had, a suave lover
visiting your nocturne, leaving before your turn, your—O!

&&&

Here's how it went down. Sam waited at the gate.
I haltered the mare with a lead line,

faster than a *No!* We snagged that horse
& away we went, like rodeo riding

but so much damn funner. Steal. Steel.
A woman's touch pulls it off.

&&&

Girls ain't tough enough to thieve.
No?
I'd say guard your wallet, Sir.
But it's already gone.

TWISTER

Laying in the tent as the funnel touches down. Can't talk.
Can't suffocate the wildfire of my brain.
Can't stop hot thoughts from clawing. Hoped
I'd grow out of it. *You'll just grow out of it*, said Mother.
Count backwards from ten eight six three E D C B A.
But I twist myself deeper into the cave of wind.
Candleflame crooning, owl-like ooOooOoo, to leave the shell
of my body in the dirt for vultures to pick clean,
new skin underneath all nerves & feeling,
no brain, no words, just worming action. Only riding,
only when Cole's arms pin me, can I breathe. I hate him
I love him can't leave him can't stay with—
his wet eyes & S-shaped neck like a heron. Dissect the bird
to see how it flies & it'll never fly again.
Every day we make choices, said Mother. *Every day.*
Hands on the keys, seeing with my
fingers. Trying to play a new rhythm,
but only one finds its spin.
Trying to think myself right
is as useless
as outrunning
the sun.
You will
always
find
you.

[FIG. 2] MEN TRY TO CONTROL WHAT THEY CANNOT UNDERSTAND.

Minor Key

"Dressed in men's clothes, riding in a good saddle, and armed with a brace of formidable pistols, Belle Starr has raided, caroused, and participated in every known form of outlawry prevalent in the nation. She rode at a pace and with a grace that new no equal. She shot with great skill, and with it all, she was a well-educated and accomplished woman. Many citizens of Fort Smith have heard her play on the piano in this city, and she was generally recognized as thoroughly well posted in various other accomplishments."
—JW Weaver's obituary of Belle Starr

Subtle shift
    Not lower
Not higher
    Sideways
Unlocking
    Sweet lies
But to whom
    About what
Meandering
    Treble
Urge & ache
    A dirge
The ear
    Only hears
As the lips
    That scored
The air
    Say *no more*

SIDESADDLE

ladies face the side !   protect   your gowns
your fineries ladylike !   ride ladies   hide yourselves
sidesaddle   nothing to straddle   nothing between your legs
except ropey heat   slick muscle   back straight as granite
calves strong enough   to choke a man   had   to peel one
off me   his tongue green as poison   expect $ would
buy an easy life   but servitude ain't easy   is it ?
grooming a buckskin   too handsome   had to steal him !
amaranth smoke   horseshit redolent as old biscuits
judge parker   i meant no harm !   wrong place !   true unstory !
wrong   time !   sidesaddle is a contortion   an idea
inherited   practice   racing   trading one name for another
think   of your grandmother   your dear mother who couldn't ride
hold the   reins   stride aside   such   horse/man/ship
leaving home behind   face the side !   leaning   into the swerve
each nerve on fire   protect   your gown   ladies !   line your lips
hip   heel   face forward   thrash your knees   kneading leather
like an axe   in your thorax   that twist   in the middle
sideriding   every inch fighting   lane of mane   faster
harder   damn it hurts   but better   than a   slow
death   the corpse breath   of   sitting   still

HARD

My favorite husband was my worst lover
        rough but tender
        whiskey-blind balladeer
My outlaw, my hard man couldn't stay
        perennial
        penance
Lips ripe as mulberries bursting on a secret branch
        Wait
        I can't
Sunbaked cheeks, leathered hands the size of saddles
        I freed him
        with one lie
After the ambush, wobbling in the dust like a speared bull
        death / bed
        blood & brine
With you have I been a real woman
        I let him die
        thinking it true
All love is tough love
        every house
        a house of cards
So shuffle hard

AIDING & ABETTING

"Belle Starr was a character. She swore and smoked and talked slang just like a man."
—*The Sunday Gazetteer. Vol 8. No 28. November 10, 1889*

No need to ask. I'd do it anyway. Over & over & over again until there was no more coin or jewel left to steal. I'd take the vault & the warped wood floor that held it erect & the house that housed it & every wood sliver that had ever cast a blessed shadow upon it. I'd steal the whole town for Jim. Then he'd owe me. Once, demon-eyed, torched with whiskey, Jim rushed me outside, his grip tight around my wrist. He balanced a red apple on my head, said *stand still*, he was gonna shoot it off.
Im gonna shoot it clean off, laughing like a five year old, so plastered on drink he cast wide ovals into the dirt with his depraved sway. Breath from his rotten backteeth as sharp & underworldly as a mummified rat. His sticky finger on the trigger. *Don't you trust me?* he asked. *Of course not.* I grabbed the red fist of apple & punched him in the head with it. Now he's gone, damn him, & still do I love him, but like a brother or a husband? I want men strong enough to follow me. Cole & his timepiece, leather, wax. Mustachioed like an ancient walrus. *Wanna ride with us*, he asked. I was but fourteen when the James guerillas started carousing at the farm, before the unfriendly war. *Strap in.* The secret to getting away with it? First, get away. We lick the salt of incinerated meat. We swim with our clothes on. We wrap ourselves in bear skin still warm with the echo of the stab. My heart is a bear heart, a ruby caked in mud. We camp under celestial chandeliers, rifles as pillows, until the flames die & we wake shivering. Jim sips whiskey for break-fast, shaking, like his hands ain't his hands. Blue Duck stands too long in the rain. Each man wants me to hold him, rock him like a baby. *Never a more hideous band of guerillas has one*

town ever seen! As the 'brains' of cattle & horse thieves,
burglars, holdup men, & other outlaws, it was her function to
secure the quickest possible release of any member of the gang
who got entangled with the law. Aiding, helping them relax in
a most intimate way. Abetting, hustling these boys at cards &
dominoes. Drinking in Robber's Cave, gambling at Younger's
Bend. Waking in the blue blink of an early frost. I watched
smoke coil over the town & knew Quantrill had massacred
them all. Foolish, the ways men pretend they will live forever.
Cole walked thirty miles in the cold. I held his feet against my
bare stomach to warm him, & his freeze branded my flesh.
I mopped the floor after he pissed himself in his sleep. Cole
shook something fierce, like a condemned man before the
firing squad. So drunk he forgot his own name. We screamed
in each other's faces. I may not know who I am supposed to
be, but with these men, my friends, I let myself see. Preacher
says, *Pledge devotion to God & thou shall live eternal.* But we
all perish, yes? Exiting this peculiar plane is a great curse of
grace. Our invitation to dust off the piano, shoot the bottle
into a thousand pieces, have a good cry & write your damn
Mother. Hold my hand & watch as the tree branch, so heavy
with ripe peaches, tells its secrets to the grass.

[FIG. 3] YOUNGER'S BEND OFFERS OUTLAWS SHELTER, WARMTH.

Séance

Can you hear me? Tap once for yes!
The medium is as convincing as a wax effigy
of the queen, but I'm in this gaslit hell
because I miss your touch, Sam, so much.
Don't care if she's lying. Love's like that—
a shared delusion, brief infusion
of insanity on which we both agree. *Myra
Maybelle*, Mother shouted, *if you run
with Jesse James & those animals,
you're gonna get yerself killed.*
She tried to scare me outta me,
her bony finger stabbing the air.
I tightened my grip on the reins, went faster.
Ever since I can remember, I tried to forget
the future. What use is it, a girl like me,
any girl at all, fighting our destiny,
blood in the dust. Why bother with crystal
balls, tarot. We slice through the gossamer
brain at some point, find our way
to the other side, whatever it takes.
Might as well drown in velvet & brocade,
ostrich feathers & millinery, hickory smoke,
whiskey-soaked town in flames. The amber
sex of it in your nose. *Caw caw kraaree*,
screams the crow. He's watching me. *Don't go.*
Wretched sideways light, clouds like bruises,
wailing, warnings spelled by fallen feathers,
phantom fathers, saliva of vultures, putrid feast.
I thought omens were meant to test me. But
they were never for me. Nothing was. Except

your tongue on mine, our bloodied muscles
after the saloon brawl. I wrote a song about it.
Remember? *Sam Starr, your widow needs you*!
The medium's got us holding hands now.
Tap if you hear us! Tap if you are near!
The séance table pulses, round
& swollen as a baby-cursed belly. *Play for me*,
you said. You loved when I pounded the keys.
What's death like, Sam, a sea of fire or
field of light, hammock of white
bright as violet candy on my tongue?
In this tomb of the charlatan's room,
can you hear me? Push through.
Tap if you can hear us, Sam Starr!
You went & ended up dead &
I wear your ghost close as this silk slip.
You put your hands on my ribcage
like you were about to crack me in half.
Tap tap tap tap. *It is I, Sam. Save yourself,*
Dear Belle. Live on. Be free! Your words ring
from everywhere & nowhere like the pastor's
bell. The medium lets go, holds her heart
as if it's about to leap through her chest.
I miss you, Husband, but I don't need your
permission now. Never did. The circle gasps,
at me, or your raspy voice. Who knows.
Look at that taxidermy bird, frozen
in flight. Don't you think I know my fate?
Speak again, Sam! the circle is chanting
Speak speak speak! roaring like the

beauty of a baby ripping through me,
hawk cry piercing the cloud line. Gals have no
_____ in this world. We have to make it.
Can you hear me, Sam, cries the medium,
her rhythm slow, melodious as the lullaby
I sang to Pearl & to you.
Wax staining the tablecloth.
Wax burning my knuckles.
That's how love is, a flood of heat,
greed, serpent eating its own tail,
a need to root, set another you loose.
More more more more more more.
Any wonder marriage is war.
Your ideas are too big for your head, you said.
Look at her, at me, the ventriloquist
with her wand of luminous paint, the trick.
Can you hear me, Sam?
No. Now you listen.
I got something say.

SLAUGHTER

after the kill
the moonless
night faceless
as a maggot

SMOKE & LEATHER

Two pleasures respectable women ain't supposed to enjoy—

Tobacco & straps—holster oiled, lips supple as raw meat—

You're outta yer mind, Sam said, *you're totally mindless*—

The saddle fits—riding faster than spitting out *I'm pregnant*—

Sweat & horse hair—my velvet pocked by cinder—

Holding reins too tight will slow a lady down—so let go—*go*

No feeling more alive than nearly dying—

Woodsmoke thick as a rope around your neck—

REPORT

Belle Starr Sighting: 5th Of August. Stay Vigilant. Keep
Hands On Weapons In Presence Of Fugitive. Look Out
For The Grand Plumed Hat & Whirl Of Purple Velvet
Skirt That Signify Starr, Belle. Sex, Female. Weight, 115
Pounds. Do Not Look Into The Convict's Obsidian Eyes,
For Even The Prison Matron & The Honorable Isaac
Parker AKA The Hanging Judge Were Charmed By Belle.
Do Not Trust. Call Local Bounty For Reprimand.

O Star-Crossed Lovers, O Happy Dagger, O

Now you're Romeo, O, throwing pebbles at my window,
carving my key into your arm.

Now you're Juliet, O, opening your dress, playing dead
to resurrect yourself later.

Now I'm Romeo, swallowed by cold as old poison rolls
down my throat, raw O.

Now I'm Juliet, O, tearing my dress, incanting *wolf!*,
watching you watch me from afar.

Now we're Romeo, raging in the tomb, a trapped storm,
& O—how we drain the vile.

Now we're Juliet, stabbing our heart with the dagger.
& O—how deep it slides.

[FIG. 4] THE PEARL—HANDLE REVOLVER TEMPTS HER HAND.

Assassin

Raptor, Cay-ote, Cougar, Bobcat, Rattlesnake, Black Widow,
Bull, Bud, Uncle, Traveling Preacher, Edgar Watson, Twist
A man who feels slighted

A man who is laughable

A man who is

[FIG. 5] BELLE STARR WAS A SNAKE OF A WOMAN. A VILE REPTILE.

Rattle

2.

Thick as the musky brine of night terrors. Let me hold her, like my own memory. Fangs sharper than the point of graphite that defines time. The snake winds into a spring, a vector, upslurred slant. **The viper is a living lighting bolt**, a writhing dagger. She feels weakness through earth.

1.

The rattlesnake smells with her mouth, makes music through her body. Movement is her instrument. Precise as a tiny skull disinterred from a prairie hawk. Hear that? Like mice in the wall, she is a bad omen. Here, **let me suck out the venom**. Lips to dusty skin. Here, let me show you.

3.

What a beauty, I said to Jim.
That rattler queen sunning
herself in the ditch, claiming
her space. Jim looked horrified,
like I spat a cannon of tobacco
juice in his face. **You're crazy!**
He stormed off with his gun.
One shot & she was splayed.
The spray of the liquid red heat
inside us all.

Ambush

"Word has been received from Eufala, Indian Territory, that
Belle Starr was killed there Sunday night."
—*New York Times*, February 6, 1889

"On February 3, 1889, two days before her 41st birthday, she was
killed. She was riding home from a neighbor's house in Eufaula,
Oklahoma when she was ambushed."
—*Los Angeles Times*, February 17, 2002

Revenge is the demand
to play another hand. Deal!

Forgive Belle. That James boys spell.
The only woman among the outlaws—

a refrain as useless as beauty, drops
of blood in the dirt, inflorescence.

A cave relies on lies,
the illusion of depth.

Ambushed! She fell off her horse, was shot again
to make sure she was dead.

Or, to erase her face.

Songbird

under the under   side of thunder   unlidded eye
  dehide truth from the trick wall of the brothel
unwind the wind on which the songbird has sung
  dewild the id from the kid
  debead the sea of its black pearl eyes & see what sinks
  deseed the apple, let the barrel ferment
unsink the ship from the swerve
  decloud daydreams from meringue light
dismantle the train robbery coin by coin

INVASIVE

Like ivy & thistle
Belle's everywhere.

You never wanted
me to be me.

Have I waited too long?
Am I too old to cry?

No one would believe.
Would anyone realize

they left me behind—
a small, unlucky lady,

face gone, half-
dead in the dirt?

[FIG. 6] BELLE STARR & HER LOVERS, HUSBANDS, KIN, NEIGHBOR.

FIRE

My insistent Mister__Husband__
        My inchoate fear__landlocked__

I've learned how to luxuriate in heat
        I've learned how to claw dirt like a seed

Every way is the only way
        I want it

FOLIE À DEUX

Following the Civil War, Maybelle "Belle" Shirley married the
outlaw Jim Reed in 1866, after having fancied him as a teen-
ager. Two years later, in 1868, Belle gave birth to her first child,
Rosie Lee (nicknamed Pearl). Her second child, James Edwin
(nicknamed Edward & Eddie), was born in 1871. Belle tried
to convince Jim Reed to try farming instead of thieving, but it
didn't take. You can't put a bowtie on a bobcat no matter how
hard you try. Jim Reed was murdered in August of 1874, in
Paris, Texas.

***

Jim, when will it end? We have a baby now. Can't you stop?
Put the bottle down. Look at each bud itching open on the tree.

.

STEADY

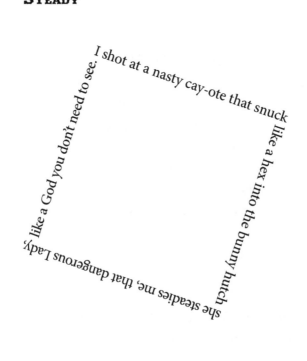

I shot at a nasty cay-ote that snuck
like a hex into the bunny hutch
she steadies me, that dangerous Lady,
like a God you don't need to see.

Voilà!

Aha! There you are, *voilà!*, Margot Douaihy thought,
I've been waiting for you, moon, & you came, but Margot
Douaihy did not think, the thought thought her, the
floating rock brought Margot Douaihy to the firmament,
voilà!, here I am, one node in the rhizome, one ember
blinking in the glowing furnace of the heart of the
intergalactic *voilà!*, it's so obvious, yes? The us-ness, the
Belle of me & the me of Belle, the id, the ego, Io's lava,
inevitable as *voilà!*, ah, all that science will reveal we
wordlessly feel: the moon is there, even when she's not,
just as the orb of eye is always awake & always asleep—
the brightest light under the darkest lid.

Dizzy

June 21, 1888

How it started: Jesse James's gang hid at her family's farm in
Missouri when lil Myra Maybelle was small enough to crawl
into a boot. Belle was but a tiny thing when she got a taste of the
outlaw way. After The War claimed her family's inn & the life of
her brother Bud—who could not carry a tune even in a bucket but
nonetheless was beloved by Belle—she turned crime dizzy. We
tried to stop her, but there is no sense-talking after a new leather
saddle & twirl of purple velvet capture you.

June 26, 1888

Hard heat. Hoed some. Hot as the hinges of Hell. Baby sick with
dizzy. We are not sleeping. John is working for Mr Adams, haying
for six days. I work for R Green, sewing brooms. I sell a broom or
two of my own, on the side like. But do not tell R Green, for I feel a
bit of an outlaw myself. My suspicions grow that Belle is riding here
in the trance of night. A strange presence, I feel, though I cannot
explain it, & though it does not have a name, untrue it does not
make. For it is clear that the hoof tracks have designed the dirt in
a pattern not unlike Belle's plumed hat with the broadest of brim.

[FIG. 7] "A STRANGE PRESENCE, I FEEL ..."

June 29, 1888

Hoed some. Hoed some more. Fainted twice from the unrelenting heat sent upwards like fields of fireweed conjured by the D-vil himself. Tracked & traced the dirt as I walked to town with the coin I have saved to buy The Paper, which, to my chagrin, reports no exploits of Belle Star. O, the deepening ache in my chest. It is an intimate & strange confusion, feeling like you know a woman whom you've not yet met.

How Not to Get Bit: A Practical Guide for Wo-men of the Plains, by Belle Starr

A cay-ote is no more than a scared dog. A cougar on the other hand, well, a cougar can & will eat you & your babies & your livestock. Trust me. Or Don't. & pay with your life.

Cougars, otherwise known as Mountainous Lions where there are mountains, not like the flat eternity of Cherokee Territory, are naturally curious animals, & that's on the near side of okay.

It is not unlikely you might see a male (alpha) cougar & a female (also alpha) in the daytime hours, near the camp, near the cave, &, in springtime, expect to see a cub or two carried helplessly by the scruff. If you don't want to get your throat slashed, your babies eaten, or your foal torn apart, stay alert when & if you encounter a troop of cougars as dusk descends.

When an alpha male wanders into view, if his head is up, if he makes eye contact, if he follows you, drink two fingers of tarantula juice, only the kind that burns, & wrestle the beast.

Don't run. That's dumb as hell.

Hold your ground. Maintain eye contact. Speak firmly, clearly.

Clap your hands if he's posturing. Throw a rock
or a tool. But not a good tool, so as to dent or ruin it.

If a particular lion keeps showing up, day after day, & he's that interested, & he tracks you, daring you to make a move, almost like a worthy opponent during a chess match, this particular lion might just be smarter than he looks, so maybe he's worth capturing & training as part of your camp or household. Pearl told me that Jinnie told her that she heard from Pastor Harper before he died that, before the war, Celia Mae in Carthage had trained a brute of a mountain lion to balance a scrap of meat on his snout, walk on his hind legs, & dance to a vaudeville tune.

Shoot to kill, never to wound.

If you do wound him, nurse that cougar back to health, & make him feel like a part of the pack, & he will be your loyal devotee for time-everlasting. Even the wildest creature wants to belong, don't it?

[FIG. 8] BELLE STARR REMAINS EXCEEDINGLY UNAFRAID.

BELLE RECEIVED A PROPER EDUCATION & BECAME A PIANIST OF HIGH REGARD

The Papers said:

> Belle leaves roses in each vault she breaks!
> Belle never steals a single jewel;
> it's rubies in triplicate or nothing at all.
> Velvet & lace, finest of petticoats.
> What else do we know? No witness
> can pin Belle's gang to a scene; they rob
> banks across county lines at the same time,
> syncing derring-do on stolen gold watches.
> In far train cars, as clocks click
> midnight, Belle & her men
> slip rings from fingers.
> Shadows unkind as guillotine blades.

WANTED

Your blazing eyes,
storm-black hair, wry smile
SAYING COME & GET ME.
But I'll never catch you.
We're too good at running
FROM WHAT WE TRULY WANT.

HEADLINE

The Fugitive Known As Belle Starr Was Born Myra Maybelle
Reeves In Carthage, Missouri, In The Year 1848 & Died By
Murder In The Year 1889. Despite Decent Bringing-Up, In
Which The Fugitive Received Proper Education & Became A
Pianist Of High Regard, Belle Starr Took To The Crime-Life
Faster Than A Vole Takes To Munching On Beans. The Fugitive
Learned To Shoot With Impressive Accuracy Before The Age
Of Fourteen, Inspired By Her Fallen Brother Bud & The Filthy
Crowd With No More Intelligence Than The Putrefaction Of
A Puddle At The Farm Near Her Family's Home In Missouri.
Farm Men Taught Belle To Cuss, Spit Tobacco Like An Oldster
At A Jerkwater Rail Stop, & Ride Her Mare As Dangerous &
Free As A Bullet Tearing Through Air. Belle Quickly Became
A Crackshot, A Rifle In Each Hand, Riding Whip Tucked Into
Her Belt, & Could Even Shoot An Acorn From A Branch With
The Slick Precision Of A Raptor Dive-Bombing A Field Mouse.
One Of Belle's First Lovers Was Cole Younger, Marauder in
the Guerilla Gang of Quantrill, A Menacing Brute Known To
Be The Bloodthirstiest Man In All Of The Outlaw Territory.
Something About Younger's Prowess Enchanted Belle, Her
Esteemed Family Legacy Replaced With A Forsaken Destiny Of
Shame. Legend Says Quantrill & His Gang Took The Lives Of
Nearly Two Hundred Innocent Persons In Lawrence, Kansas,
While Savagely Robbing The Town. Legends Suggest That Belle
Starr Was Besotted With Both Jesse James & Brawny Quantrill
But Indeed Her True Love Was Cole Younger, The Father Of
Young Pearl. The Cousin Of Jesse James, Cole Younger Rode
Off & Left Belle Broken-Hearted, Her Casket-Dark Eyes
Blazing For The Rest Of Her UnNatural Life. After The Lawless
Layabout Jim Reed—Belle's First Of At Least Six

Lawful & Unlawful "Husbands" Of Whom We Know—Shot A
Man, He & Belle, The Petticoat Terror Of The Plains, Went On
The Lam: Robbing, Bribing, Rustling Horses, & Quite Regular
Counterfeiting, Most Convincing. & Why Did The Fugitive Do
It, You Might Ask? What Would Possess A Woman To Leave
Luxury Behind For A Tatteredly Life Of Crime, Dastardly
Raids, In The Company of Malodorous Men Who Bathed With
Animal-Fat Soap In The Rain? Well, Some Say It Was As Simple
As Her Face, That Belle Starr Had An Ease & A Grace Whilst
Riding Her Horse With A Smile That Blazed Brighter Than A
Burning Barn. But Who's To Say?

"Belle Starr, Belle Starr, tell me where you have gone
Since old Oklahoma's sandhills you did roam?
Is it Heaven's wide streets that you're tying your reins
Or singlefooting somewhere below?"
—Woody Guthrie, *Belle Starr*

THE BALLAD OF BELLE STARR

BANDIT QUEEN: I
am an ember, panther murder-
er. Could have slit your throat,
burned your stagecoach
instead. Air purring,
musk of sex & sinew.

FEMALE JESSE JAMES: I
been riding since I was a teen.
Go where I want when I want.
Women take men's names
on wedding days, but we
make 'em pay & pay &—.

PETTICOAT TERROR OF THE PLAINS: I
look fine today wouldn't you say
in my brocade & hat, black
as a widow's tooth. I will not
apologize for my filigree of vanity.
You'll die naked. Not I.

VILE REPTILE: I
study my reflection
in the tobacco tin, stick
out my dusty tongue,
lizard bumped, before
spitting in the judge's eye.

TELEGRAM

DECEMBER THE 1ST

DEAR BROTHER DID YOU SEE HER DID YOU SEE HER YOU SAW
HER RIGHT O YOU HAVENT SEEN HER YET GOD ALMIGHTY WHAT
ARE YOU WAITING FOR YOU HAVE TO GET ON YER HORSE & RIDE
TO THE TERRITORIES & SEE HER SHE MAY NOT BE HERE MUCH
LONGER GET TO THE SHOW HURRY SHE IS CALLED BELLSTARR

DECEMBER THE 22ND

DEAR BROTHER I DECLARE SHE IS AN ANGEL THE MOST UNUSUAL
WOMAN I HAVE SEEN OR MAYBE HAVE EVER SEEN NOT SEEN BUT
EXPERIENCED LIKE THE MOMENT IN CHURCH WHEN YOU FEEL
A HOLY STORM INSIDE YOUR VEINS NOT THAT I AM PROPOSING
NONWORSHIPFUL NOTIONS BUT NO WORDS SATISFY & THESE
TELEGRAMS ARE EXPEN$IVE BUT YOU MUST NOT MISS HER SO
SEE HER PROMISE   NOW   GO

///

Y. What do you mean you don't know
X. Just what I said I don't know
Y. But what made you ride all the way from the border &
appear here at my tent of hypnosis
X. I don't know
Y. Okay let's start at the beginning
X. The beginning
Y. The beginning
X. I don't remember the beginning

Y. Well try maybe that's why you are here seeing that I am the greatest hypnotist that has ever lived or ever will live

X. Then why are you in this shitty tent at this crummy fair in this pit of a town

Y. Just tell me why you are here & what you need hypnosis for

X. I don't remember

Y. For crying out

X. I don't have amnesia for God's sake

Y. So you're telling me you truly don't know why you're here

X. You tell me

Y. Okay you just showed up here hollering something about a bell & you want to recall every detail *bell bell* you yelled

Y. Belle Starr you mean

X. Well I don't you know you raced in on your horse screaming *bell bell bell bell bell* then you fainted

Y. Oh my god it happened to me just like my brother said

X. What happened to you

Y. I saw her I saw Belle Starr she's real she's

I Regard Myself As A Woman Who Has Seen Much Of Life

Full thunder again & O! The storm is raging down, wind tearing the tent like a terror of vultures. Dearest, I am mirthfully sick after a jackpot night. (They did manage to shoot the hat off my head as we escaped – pure luck on the part of dopey Sergeant Spade.) You should have heard their wild trills after the hit. *It's the blasted Belle Starr*! Did they ever yelp *hoo hoo* like their trousers were acid. We powered through the gate in our grand parade. Where are you? We must be on Week Four of silence, last I checked. Do you know how to reach me at xx.x.x? You must know. I will attempt to close my eyes in a nap before we set out again. I feel at the top of this arrangement, but I must admit how tired this all makes me. They keep reminding me that I am a desperate woman taking to gunfighting & gambling & robbing as if I would or could forget, & did you know they even wrote on a poster that 115 pounds is the weight of me & *O, how can she ride that mare being such a button of a fe-male*? But do they not know that in science it is the small that always takes the big. Water carves rock. It is the near-invisible instructions inside the insides that write the color of the eye & predilection for purple & fondness for thieving. It is not wise to discount the diminutives among us. I do believe I frighten the lawmen with my bold ways, or I simply confuse them – either way, they want to lock me away as if I were a mad dog or cursed doll. How I do long until I see you again? I can picture you now, those roving wolf eyes, your particular smile. Your hands dry & red as cured meat from the unfortunate wind, the ruinous force of it all. Come down here! You better! x. xx. xx x..x. (Trust you can understand my secret code. We both know the bastards at the Depot are reading my correspondence.)

[FIG. 9] THE SPIN OF A CYCLONE PULLS EVERYTHING IN.

DELICATE

The lake
          faint with
                    blue-
          bells,
perfume
          of pitted
                    fruit.
          Ache as
bare &
          delicate as
                    a wasp's
          waist—
the glue
          between
                    mind &
          movement.
A wasp's
          heart
                    lives
          in its
skin.
          I too
                    know
          how
to live
          inside
                    out.

No need
>> to sleep
>>>> or
>> fear,
roaring
>> down
>>>> what-
>> ever
road
>> you
>>>> wish.

She Stared at Nothing & Talked to Herself So Often People Wondered if She Was in a Trance, or Possessed by the D-vil Himself

She heard notes no one else heard. Saw refrains hiding in other sounds. This was as unexceptional as day turning into night.

A peculiar gal, said her cousins, friends, lovers, neighbors, & archenemies* as she faced the window, looking out, studying a field of nothing, endless prairie, space relentlessly empty, without nary a ripple of wind to disrupt the wheat.

Townsfolk wondered.

O, how they worried.

Townsfolk tried to bring her back to herself. Snap her out of it.

Sometimes, as she stared, she thought about a new dress she might buy, or a new hat she might steal, the most elegant millinery with the most luscious of brim. Sometimes she conjured a scene as simple & clean as warm butter steam escaping from a fresh biscuit. Sometimes she ran scenes of riding to Carthage, to Kansas City, to Eufala. She even thought what her horse thought, for she knew her ink-black mare's mind turned a fierce, sometimes awful script. Tis the way of the most devoted of creatures—the hardest to break, the most resistant, but when broken, they are yours & yours alone, but O, that whir of wildness remains.

You playing with my mind or something?, her husband** said more than asked, without really understanding the words he was verbalizing or the motivation for the accusation masquerading as a question.

Just thinking, she replied without turning her head.

Playing.

She had not played a proper tune in years, but the frenzied music still twitched in her mind.

There was once a time she found music so beautiful it hurt to hear it. It made her want to play. Stalk the sky until you become the hawk, she told herself. Tap the membrane until you become the rain. To play was to make something where there was absolutely nothing, like rare & complicated birdsong suddenly erupting where no birds could be seen, or a stubborn weed reaching up through the dust, ravenous vines, like time, that strangle Mother's flowers but can cure a fever if you boil them just right.

* Belle Starr's covetous neighbor & tenant, Edgar Watson. In the undesirable occurrence you must shake hands with him before buying his unfortunate corn, you will no doubt feel that his fingers are thick with grime. & crime.

** The lawless degenerate bootlegger gunslinger thief Sam Starr who was so devastatingly handsome with his hard jaw & broad chest like a bank vault, Belle Starr became his & his alone. Most of the time. Some of the time.

ONE BLADE OF SHADE IN THE RAGING RAGING SUN

                                              is all you get
                                                one hand

                                         on the saddlehorn
                                                one hand

                                                   up high
                                                   ` ` ` `

                                         going or coming?
                                       don't need to know

if an osprey swallowed the moon,
would she burn inside like a firefly?

my ear to the lightning tree
to hear your heart

roots like shooting stars
restless as we are

                                        whisper of air kiss
                                            crimson sting

                                   ` ` ` ` ` `tears that haven't
                                               formed yet

                                   dried pine like a ribcage
                                          body in supine

how can I ever
go back?

a life easy to some
impossibly numb

don't look don't look don't you're
bleedi

n

g

o

u

t

DOUBLE EXPOSURE

DOUBLE EXPOSURE

I wasn't in the mood for Blue Duck's mood. I was never in the mood. I jumped out of the stagecoach, alighting at Reunion Circle. There's too much to see, & I couldn't risk being seen, so I walked briskly, taking two steps at a time, almost knocked a charlatan down because he didn't move out of my way. Smiling like a jackal, smug as jackal too, making a penny here a penny there on his ridiculous "spirit" photography & elixirs that would as soon as strip the wallpaper from a brothel than fix your insides. Scoundrels are good at making you think they have answers. Some questions have no answers at all. Still, we do it, we posture, make our own myths. From Treeline Avenue to Main Street, I sprinted. I could feel eyes on me, shadowing me. My hat, one grain of privacy in the dusty street. Finally, at the house. But I didn't want to be alone. I didn't know where I wanted to be. Two places at once. Three? When you're in two worlds, you're living in none.

I wasn't in the mood—apparently. I followed myself jumping from the stagecoach, alighting at Reunion Circle. I ran to catch up with myself—never easy in my dress. Do I always move so fast? From behind, my raven hair looks as generic as a washbasin. Even with so much to see, I burrowed my eyes down. I watched me ignore the smiling charlatan selling snake oil & haunted photos. We turned left, me following me, from Treeline Avenue to Main Street. My Monday face as pallid as the bottomless cup of a skeleton's eye socket. Black-brimmed hat providing a partition between me & me. During the slow ascent upstairs—one foot, other foot—too absorbed to notice me following me. What if women said hello to ourselves, hugged ourselves more? Would we hold onto each other? Reaching not just for hands but the tender & bruised parts, the broken places? Or would it pierce the membrane & let the spirits go, like two cracks of one flash revealing the ghost?

GRAVE

Shed not for her the bitter tear,
Nor give the heart to vain regret
Tis but the casket that lies here,
The gem that filled it sparkles yet.
—Belle Starr's tombstone, Muskogee County, Oklahoma

How serious your voice
when the news is ungood.
Clouds light as the laugher
I hear less & less these days.
Punishing winds.
Police posters
everywhere now.
The tomb is one room
we need not decorate,
not that I have refinement
or skill in that domain.
All flames die.
Though, even
the furthest star
will reach the
lake of the eye

                eventually.

Scorpion Like a Constellation of

A face of no face

It's night. It's day. All I know about you is everything. My children are not my own. My children are not children at all, old souls since the day they were born, Pearl & Eddie. I am dead. I am alive. The empress scorpion gives birth live, a live birth, a writhing mass, a disaster of light. Thick grit "rid hard & put away wet"—that's what they say about me. Why? Cause I aint a doll they can throw against the wall.

Scorpio light

Impressive weapon of body   honed for predation

I am a star, Starr, stare hard

Exoskeletal

Frantic shadows   two bella moths sparring

Where you kissed me smolders, still

a small fire burning under the snow

[FIG. 10] VENOMOUS EMPRESS SCORPION.

THE KILLER

"He has a villainous eye, an idiot's head, and I believe—a satanic heart. I hate him without a reason, yet hate is reason enough for its own being."
—Edgar Watson as described by Richard K. Fox

Edgar Watson[1]
    son
    father
dirt farmer
    Belle Starr's
    tenant, remnant
lye & gunpowder
    horror of
    vermillion
jugular pump
    no prison
    as heavy
as heartbreak
    a nothing man
    castration
Edgar Watson[2]
    asked Belle [   ]
    Belle said [   ]

---

[1] "Watson was charged but never tried. There was simply not enough evidence to empanel a jury."
—*Oklahoma Scoundrels*

[2] "Watson was tried, convicted and executed by hanging for the murder."
— Frank Boardman "Pistol Pete" Eaton

rank foam
      of an outhouse
      overflowing
don't laugh, ladies
      a weak man
      bites when hurt
rattlesnake skin
      wound tight
      with clues,
oscillate
      kaleidoscope
      tube of obfuscation
tiny windows
      collide, stars
      blur into blood

BLOOD & VELVET

To live well is to love what leaves. The same surprise. The blackjack tree's wild crown, each leaf thick as the leather cover of a book too rare to open. The laughter of a redstart. The moon distant as the inside of a marble. Why can't it stay longer—the electric storm, this prairie light? Smoke in my hair from a good fire. Everything feels silken as I dance: memories of you, the scent of your neck, like cold water, sawdust, & velvet. Your letters that hold me like barbed wire. The guns on my belt. Ever wonder why a hawk has no need for apologies, no choice but to take what she wants? One bird tears another other bird apart, storm-dune of blood & feathers, & in so doing, one creature's mouth against another's neck becomes a duet, the way a gun wears your hand as you fire it.

[FIG. 11] A TRUE PREDATOR DECIDES WHAT IT TAKES & WHEN.

SURVIVAL IS THE MARRIAGE OF FORGETTING & REMEMBERING

The idea that fish once walked on land cracks me up.
Every time I drink, I choke a little (my gills still intact).
What if time rewrote us, returned us to the sludge?
How far have we come? Even in death, I can't sleep.
Igneous rock probably dreams better than I do.
We like rivers & mud, me & the land-water creatures.
Such pluck, such daring as the frog tries to escape
from the needle-sharp beak of the leggy heron.

Re-Member

If a memory changes
every time it's recalled,

what I'm remembering
never happened. Not really.

I've replayed our affair—night
ride, bonfire—one hundred times.

Does that mean our story
has changed one hundred times?

A memory isn't a picture pinned
to the corkboard of the mind.

It's stone revised by water,
tides, tiny scrapes of why.

Memories of movement are encoded
in muscle, but muscle is memory.

When I remember you tonight,
will you ride away, or stay?

MYSTERY

July 1, 1888

Walked to Owasso & back. Mother watched Baby who is still
sick. It is ten miles there, ten miles back. Traded butter for
clover. Used the hoe to kill the vole. At night we washed. John
threshed for Mr Powell. I read just about everything I could re-
garding the character of Belle Starr who we saw riding through
town last year. One sighting & forget her I am unable. I read &
read & John threshed & threshed until his limbs burned whilst
inside of me blossomed a different kind of yearning. A new
vole appeared. I clutched the hoe. John asked me to wash him
and I said nothing. We asked Mr Powell if he had heard of new
exploits of Belle Starr & her young paramour, Jim July Starr,
nee Jim July. Nope, he replied. No more tales of your Belle, said
he with a side eye of bemusement. Whelp, I was taken quite
back. My Belle? What a thought indeed.

July 16, 1888

Hoed & hoed some more. Broke the hoe. Went to T Trout & got
new hoe. All forenoon Baby cried. Sick with the dizzy again. To
kill a squirrel, I imagine Belle Starr's gun resting on her strong
shoulder which had the immediate effect of steadying me.
Pleasant afternoon of sewing brooms. Forenoon Mercury hit
95. Hotter than a billy goat in a pepper patch. To survive Baby's
screams, I imagine Belle Starr's gun poised as elegantly as a
parrot on a pirate. Went to sell a broom to T Trout whose hogs
are dropping off with some new disease. Mr Reeves said that
because Belle has emptied one too many banks with no

disguise upon her face, most likely she would be shot in the back. Though she criminalizes, I would rather Belle not get shot in the back. Sister held a quilting. We, Mother, & D (that newcomer), helped quilt. Incorporating a purple tile on the quilt was my idea.

March 20, 1889

Windy to-day. Mended a shoe & sewed a broom. Baby still sick with dizzy. I am most ill myself, reading about the cowardly killing of Belle Starr. The Paper prints very few details about her death. And very often one or two of the details contradict one or two of them other details and I am most unsure of what is true and what is untrue. It appears that Belle Starr's death remains unsolved, a mystery as peculiar as the sinister spin of a tornado. But, if you ask me, most surely the killer is Belle's covetous neighbor, Edgar Watson. In the undesirable occurrence you must shake hands with Watson for one reason or another, you will no doubt feel that his fingers are still hot with shot. As dis- agreeable it might be to thieve, or harbor hard men, it is tough going out here, most definite for a lady.

April 4, 1889

For certain Belle Starr had her addictions: to fleeing & finery, purple velvet skirts & hats with the broadest of brim & feathers of the ostrich, a rare bird indeed. Now you tell me: How was she 'spected to get them? You know the saying: no lard unless you boil the hog.

Robber's Cave

                    is a burrow, a hole,
oval of socket after the eyeball's
gouged out. The war saw
no shortage of barbarity.
She discovered the cave with her nose,
chewing the air like a mourning dove.
After she watched union soldiers rip
her brother's hair, whip her horse,
strip her mother. She crushed a bird
holding it too tight.
Thought she was helping.
Or didn't. Safe now.
The new her,
hiding the men.
Not that any secret stays
where you bury it.

[FIG. 12] ROBBER'S CAVE, A HAVEN OF SHADOWS.

Lacuna

They say Belle's on the move, riding here, consorting there,
tearing it up with the wretches the criminals the gangbangers
the bad boys. The rogues she adored, their skin like rough
crystals. Who on God's good earth would imagine such a
demure gal would find company with miscreants & lice, the
townsfolk refrained. A life on the run. But isn't a Goddess
is always starving in Hades, banished by some jealous man,
eternally one wisp away from touching the ripe fruit? What
about the lake of starfire that holds me invisibly as a song? My
heart has a hole, the size of locket hiding the face of a woman
who once pressed her ear to my chest, a woman I will never
marry.

BRIDLE

The bridle is what holds the bit

The bit is what gives the horse direction

The bridle gives control of the horse to the rider

The bridle places force on the most sensitive places
of the horse's face

The only relief from the pressure of the bit is to submit

The "bridle" is a way to say "pressure"

Only a broken horse can be controlled

The only relief from the force of the bit is to submit

One bit of freedom will ruin a horse

Broke

I Fall to Pieces on Price
Chopper's radio & I can't move,
can't find my wallet to pay
for the coffee beans & juniper beer
neatly bagged by the nose-ringed cashier.
The song's swing, bite like a broken string,
a voice so raw even Belle Star would cry.
Nose-ring says, *Pay tomorrow.*
I've been broke, too. I trust you.
But I'm half-listening, thinking
about Belle & Blue Duck. Outlaw
weddings. & us, slow dancing
in high heels, how we never
had a chance. Like the gay cowboys
in the movie—the short talky one
& the tall quiet one.
They have spouses & houses,
but every year they meet
where they first met.
& in their minds they are there,
always there,
like gold dust under river rocks,
where it's always summer,
even in winter.
Love you can't do a damn
thing about, except
let it in,
let it be beautiful
as it breaks you apart.

THE THROAT IS THE SONG

Dusk, bliss of weightlessness.

The crepuscular slice where prairie meets sky,

slim hinge between this world and the next.

All the people who have come before us.

All the people who will follow.

No math, no map can track it.

But if you squint just right, everything fits.

It is a puzzle, a miracle, how tides work, how time works?

The air, sweet & dry as hay.

The song is the throat.

The way you feel near a person is the person.

Silence is its own way to listen.

If you tilt your ear just right,

you can hear

her.

A Dangerous Woman

Who am I? The spontaneous calculus. Ecstatic map you
will never understand. Belle Starr, a crack shot. Hot-headed
temptress, murdered in cold blood by a salty neighbor or
jealous ex or castigated son or the cruel duel of stolen land.

My name is Belle Starr. My name was Belle Starr. **Born 1848.
Died 1889.** That's what the disruptions of stone reveal. & yet I
feel so alive laying here in this bath of red dirt, my lovers crying
my name, beating their chests. Is there any hurt as piercing as
pain of those left behind? In death, past the material mem-
brane, my purple glamor flattened like an ant under a boot, but
I admit it's easier to move about unnoticed, like wearing a suit
made of rain.

Who am I but a woman destined to be mourned. Adore me!
Adorn my grave with heather, goldenrod, tall grasses, crimson-
dipped feathers of crows deboned by prairie hawks. Stalks of
predation. **You ~~don't~~ know my face.** You've read about me
in the pages of the *National Police Gazette*. You've heard my
name glinting like sonic diamonds in the whispers of bordello
hooligans & the lice of the sand dunes.

Who am I but Belle Starr, the Petticoat Terror of the Plains.
Now I am as small as the pollen that feeds petaled things, as
wild as the gully washer that drowns your echo. I might be
gone but **I will forever haunt you, a heart murmur, broken
from the inside out.**

"The outlaw hero must die so the civilized man may live."
You hated that I rode faster than the boys. Siren, vixen, whore,
horse thief—that's me. Too clever for my own good.

Holy smokes, Sherriff, we lost her again! You lost me? **As if I
were yours to lose?** Though Jim & Sam & Cole & Blue Duck &
Middleton & Jim July lost me too. Love is a double bind. Every
heart is a bird throwing itself against its cage, hammering the
delicate ribs, desperate to escape. *I love you*, you say. *I'm in love
with you*, but love is neither a place nor state (perhaps of mad-
ness). *You ain't bad*, we say in the cowboy way.

Who am I but the needles in your legs when you ride too long.
Shake it out, shake it out. **I am the original sin & the rebirth**, the
volcanic skin of the deep wound, tonguing the pool in the gums
were the tooth got knocked out after I shot up the saloon.

Who am I but Belle Starr alias Bella Starr, Queen of the Ban-
dits, Myrabelle Shirley Starr. Contradictions, convulsions, like
the delirious eyes of a hypnotized man—his electric jelly—the
twinned lakes that **see in the dark**. Isn't that what we do when
we dream?

Who am I but a woman who simply wanted to live, to ride, **to
feel lightning inside**. How could I ever stay still & knit? Hold
your rage & your praise. Kiss me instead.

Legend says I, Belle Starr, crossed lines of friend & lover. Indeed, I was enticed by the debonair outlaw Blue Duck, who could ride backwards & shoot blindfolded & sing a lilting croon like a whip-poor-will. I was a **most unconventional woman** who smiled at grief & smelled as gnarly as the char of a burned wagon, yet I melted into men's lips, so slim & willing as harp strings vibrating in song.

Who am I but **a wild bird inured to pain**. I'm dead. I must be dead. I'm alive. I've never felt so light. The ache to feel awake, my whole life, gnawing & clawing my secret self free. I'm Belle Starr. Three days shy of 41 years old. I married six men, traded the fineries of a decent marriage, thank you, for a life in the shadows, except it's my show. Isn't living for the alive?

Who am I but the eternal ear. I hear them still: *The lawless dame Belle Starr was killed today, bled out from two gunshots wounds—one to the back of the heart, one bullet to the face.* Was the killer the son, Eddie, or the daughter, Pearl? A rageful ex-lover? Can't recall exactly, but please note the menace of my disgraced neighbor, Watson, & how men insist on having the last word. O, poor her, they prattle on, the infamous Belle, a decaying carcass in the dust. But **even in sediment, an iridescence whisper**s: we were whole.

Who am I but ink. Silk. Milk. Mink. Watch how I refuse to sink. *Belle Starr was the very worst and very best, more amorous, more relentless, braver than Joan of Ark.* Look at her! I'm a **fox licking my wounds by the fire**, but you can't stop staring, can you?

[FIG. 14] ONLY A COWARD SHOOTS A LADY IN THE BACK.

Who am I but the miracle of being loved & left, to be inside a body then outside. To hold someone, be held by them. In the leaving you feel their shape. I am the widow, the window of hell, lick of the church bell, Belle Starr, the tickle in your ear, **your fear that you will never own me, never control any woman.**
I am the chrysalis cracking, the riding whip snapping, burning down the home that was not my own, fleeing a life that was never mine.

Who am I but a **woman who chose, a varicose ghost.** To run, to be on the run, fireball of sun, the haze of undone, your fever dream of what could be. A heart torn in half is the color of a flame. A flame is a name that roars to life in a memory.

Who am I?

[FIG. 15] A WOMAN OF MYSTERY KILLED, BUT HER STORY LIVES ON.

AFTERWORD

Bandit/Queen is a docupoetic project exploring Belle Starr,
a notorious Wild West outlaw, and her unsolved murder in
1889. Belle Starr traded a privileged upbringing for a life on
the lam—marrying outlaws, thieving, and providing shelter for
criminal gangs, all with her signature brocade and purple hats.
After the media locked into her story, Belle Starr rocketed to
fame. She "became" a compelling anti-hero, icon, and criminal
mastermind—The Female Jesse James. But who was Belle
Starr? Where do fiction and fact overlap?

Everyone from journalists to filmmakers have imagined Belle
Starr, but stories about her have mostly been created and
distributed through patriarchal lenses. The tall tales about Belle
are so elaborate and widespread, it is still difficult to divine fact
from fiction. Some of the extreme fabrications include Belle
Starr ruthlessly raiding villages, dressing as a man to fight a
bull, masquerading as a preacher, and killing a panther.

Here's what we know for sure: Belle Starr was born as Myra
Belle Shirley in Carthage, Missouri in 1848, into an established
family and aristocratic upbringing that she later repudiated
for an outlaw life. She gained notoriety with her impressive
sidesaddle horsewomanship, velvet garments, ornately
feathered hats, as well as her gambling, drinking, and pair of
six-shooters she wore on a cartridge belt. Belle had at least six
male partners, mostly outlaws. Debate still simmers (in Woody
Guthrie's ballad, Belle Starr had eight lovers), but historians
tend to agree that she consorted with (in alphabetical order):
Blue Duck, Jim July, who eventually took the surname of Starr,
John Middleton, Sam Starr, Cole Younger, and Jim Reed. Belle

bore two children, Pearl and Edward. Legends purport that Belle Starr was a stone-cold killer and a cut-throat gang leader, but court records reveal that she was arrested only once, for horse theft, and was sentenced to six months of prison time on two counts.

Belle Starr was killed by an unknown assailant on February 3, 1889, shot twice—once in the back and once in the face and neck. In one retelling, a man named Edgar Watson, allegedly Belle Starr's tenant-farmer, was charged for the crime but never tried.

Belle Starr's murder has never been solved, nor have many questions surrounding her motivations.

In this book, we are interested in interrogating Belle Starr's story from a feminist perspective, taking artistic license to channel the essence of this complex woman. For more than a century, Belle Starr's persona was exploited to sell spurious stories that fit pre-conceived notions of transgressive femininity. We hope to offer a nuanced counterweight to the caricature.

This project was fueled by archival materials and resources housed at the Library of Congress, the University of Oklahoma Libraries Western History Collections, and the Pioneer Woman Museum in Ponca City, Oklahoma. Our work was also informed by archival research into 19th- and 20th-century books, newspapers, journals, and documents.

We dedicate this book to Belle Starr.

ACKNOWLEDGEMENTS

Deep appreciation to John Morgenstern, Editor of Clemson University Press, and Alison Mero, Managing Editor of Clemson University Press, for believing in this project. We appreciate your enduring support, incisive insights, and generosity.

Sincere thanks to Jacquelyn Slater Reese, Associate Professor of Bibliography and Librarian, Western History Collections, University of Oklahoma Libraries, for the assistance. Additional thanks to Matthew Garcia of the Western History Collections.

Gratitude to the following journals where these poems originally appeared:

"O Star-Crossed Lovers, O Happy Dagger, O!," *The West Review*

"Voila," *SunSpot Lit*

Notes

While this book of documentary poetry was inspired by historical facts, *Bandit / Queen: The Runaway Story of Belle Starr* does not purport to be a history book. We hope this project inspires a deep dive into Belle Starr's life and the complex realities of 19th-century women.

The area(s) colloquially known as the "Wild West" and Great Plains inhabited by Indigenous Nations and Affiliated Tribes, some as the result of injurious governmental relocation policies and forced displacements. The authors recognize the historical connection the archival materials have with Indigenous communities. We acknowledge and respect the diverse Indigenous peoples connected to this land and Belle Starr's story.

Most of our poems and illustrations were informed or influenced by archival materials housed at the United States Library of Congress and the University of Oklahoma Libraries Western History Collections. We found these archives particularly inspiring during our research and drafting processes: the William M. Tilghman and Zoe A. Tilghman Collection, the Edna Gaither Collection, the Waddie Hudson Collection, and Charles B. Rhodes Collection.

Sources & Archives Referenced

Map, "Indian Territory, with part of the adjoining state of Kansas, &c."; Contributor Names: United States. Army. Corps of Topographical Engineers. Created / Published: Washington, D.C.: Engineer Bureau, War Dept., 1866. Repository: Library of Congress Geography and Map Division Washington, D.C. 20540-4650 USA dcu; Control Number: 2011590003

University of Oklahoma Libraries' Western History Collections: Zoe A. Tilghman Collection; Folder 19: Traylor, Leslie (December 13, 1934). Letter to Zoe Tilghman, re: Belle Starr, William Stiles, Jim Reed, and James-Younger gangs.

University of Oklahoma Libraries' Western History Collections: Waddie Hudson Photograph Collection. Prints of outlaws.

University of Oklahoma Libraries' Western History Collections: William Matthew Tilghman Collection. Papers, 1843-1960. Clippings regarding "Starr, Belle" and outlaws.

University of Oklahoma Libraries' Western History Collections: Charles B. Rhodes Collection. Papers, 1864-1950.

University of Oklahoma Libraries' Western History Collections: Edna Gaither Collection & Pamphlets, 1860-1956.

Chicago School of Poetics: Documentary Poetry www.chicagoschoolofpoetics.com/documentary-poetics

OTHER KEY CITATIONS & REFERENCES

"I am a friend to any brave and gallant outlaw."
—Belle Starr's words as reported in *Oklahoma Scoundrels: History's Most Notorious Outlaws, Bandits & Gansters*, Robert Barr Smith & Laurence J. Yadon, p 17 (Charleston, SC: The History Press, 2016)

"Court records show that in July 1882, she and her husband, Sam Starr, were arrested for stealing a horse from Pleasant Andrew."

— Jonita Mullins, *Oklahoma Originals: Early Heroes, Heroines, Villains & Vixens* (Charleston, SC: The History Press, 2019), pp. 124-125.

"Dressed in men's clothes, riding in a good saddle, and armed with a brace of formidable pistols, Belle Starr has raided, caroused, and participated in every known form of outlawry prevalent in the nation. She rode at a pace and with a grace that new no equal. She shot with great skill, and with it all, she was a well-educated and accomplished woman. Many citizens of Fort Smith have heard her play on the piano in this city, and she was generally recognized as thoroughly well posted in various other accomplishments."
—JW Weaver's obituary of Belle Starr, as presented in the book *Belle Starr* by Burton Roscoe (NY, NY: Random House, 1941), p. 123.

"Mother Nature was indulging in one of her rarest freaks when she produced such a novel specimen of woman kind"
—Richard K. Fox, *Bella Starr; The Bandit Queen, or The Female Jesse James* (Austin, TX: The Steck Company, 1889) Reissued in the book *Bella Starr; or The Bandit Queen* (Austin, TX: The Steck Company, 1960)

"He has a villainous eye, an idiot's head, and I believe—a satanic heart. I hate him without a reason, yet hate is reason enough for its own being."
—Richard K. Fox, *Bella Starr; The Bandit Queen, or The Female Jesse James* (Austin, TX: The Steck Company, 1889) Reissued in the book Bella Starr; or The Bandit Queen (Austin, TX: The Steck Company, 1960)

"Belle stood out in her velvet riding habits riding sidesaddle. ... Even so, Belle often won these competitions and was a big draw to visitors who came to see her compete."
—Jonita Mullins, *Oklahoma Originals: Early Heroes, Heroines, Villains & Vixens* (Charleston, SC: The History Press, 2019), p. 125.

"Belle was, in the parlance of the common criminal underworld, a 'fix,' that is, some one who had the knack and intelligence and cash to get at the right persons among the administrators of the law and arrange nolle prosses, paroles, releases, pardons, verdicts, and suspended or light sentences. As the 'brains' of cattle and horse thieves, burglars, holdup men, and other outlaws, it was her function to secure the quickest possible release of any member of the gang who got entangled with the law."
—Burton Rosco, *Belle Starr* (NY, NY: Random House, 1941), pp. 195-196.

"On February 3, 1889, two days before her 41st birthday, she was killed. She was riding home from a neighbor's house in Eufaula, Oklahoma when she was ambushed. After she fell off her horse, she was shot again to make sure she was dead. Her death resulted from shotgun wounds to the back and neck and in the shoulder and face. Legend says she was shot with her own double-barrel shotgun."
—Rasmussen, Cecilia (February 17, 2002). "L.A. Then and Now: Truth Dims the Legend of Outlaw Queen Belle Starr". *Los Angeles Times*. Archived from the original on March 6, 2016. Retrieved January 23, 2013.

According to Frank Eaton, Edgar Watson was tried, convicted, and executed by hanging for the murder: https://web.archive.org/web/20160306045246/http://articles. latimes.com/2002/feb/17/local/me-then17

"Tucked in the southeast corner of Oklahoma, past the beautiful vistas of Lake Eufaula is a peaceful, yet adventurous place. Described as a relaxing hideaway in the land of the outlaws, Robbers Cave State Park gets its name from the hideout for a notorious group of bandits storied to be led by the outlaw Jesse James and other desperados in cahoots with local outlaw Belle Starr."
—*Metro Family Magazine*

"Belle Starr was a character. She swore and smoked and talked slang just like a man."
—*The Sunday Gazetteer.*Vol 8. No 28. November 10, 1889

CPSIA information can be obtained
at www.ICGtesting.com
Printed in the USA
JSHW031919130622
27024JS00003B/216